A PRACTICAL GUIDE TO GEOMANTIC DIVINATION

SMALL GEMS BY
DR. ISRAEL REGARDIE

Other Titles by Dr. Israel Regardie

A Garden of Pomegranates
A Practical Guide to Geomantic Divination - A Small Gem
Attract and Use Healing Energy - A Small Gem
Be Yourself - A Guide to Relaxation and Health
Ceremonial Magic
Dr. Israel Regardie's Definitive Work on Aleister Crowley,
  The Eye In The Triangle
Healing Energy, Prayer and Relaxation
How To Make and Use Talismans - A Small Gem
My Rosicrucian Adventure
Mysticism, Psychology and Oedipus - A Small Gem
Teachers of Fulfillment
The Art and Meaning of Magic - A Small Gem
The Body-Mind Connection, A Path to Well-Being - A Small Gem
The Complete Golden Dawn System of Magic
The Complete Golden Dawn System of Magic Book 1 - Ltd. Edition
The Complete Golden Dawn System of Magic Book 2 - Ltd. Edition
The Complete Golden Dawn System of Magic - The Black Edition
The Eye in the Triangle: An Interpretation of Aleister Crowley
The Golden Dawn Audio CDs, Vol. 1, Vol. 2, and Vol. 3
The Legend of Aleister Crowley
The Magic of Israel Regardie
The Middle Pillar
The Philosopher's Stone
The Portable Complete Golden Dawn System of Magic
The Tree of Life
The Wisdom of Israel Regardie - Vol. I
  Selected Introductions, Prefaces and Forewords
The Wisdom of Israel Regardie - Vol. II
  Selected Essays and Commentaries
The Wisdom of Israel Regardie - Vol. III
  Selected Articles, Introductions, Prefaces and Forewords
What You Should Know About the Golden Dawn
Wilhelm Reich, His Theory And Techniques
Aha! (Dr. Israel Regardie and Aleister Crowley)
Roll Away The Stone/The Herb Dangerous
  (Dr. Israel Regardie and Aleister Crowley)

MANY OF OUR TITLES AVAILABLE ON KINDLE!
Please visit our website at http://www.newfalcon.com

A PRACTICAL GUIDE TO GEOMANTIC DIVINATION

SMALL GEMS BY
DR. ISRAEL REGARDIE

NEW FALCON PUBLICATIONS
Los Angeles, California, U.S.A.

Copyright © 2017 New Falcon Publications

All rights reserved. No part of this book,
in part or in whole, may be reproduced, transmitted,
or utilized, in any form or by any means, electronic or mechanical,
including photocopying, recording, or by any information storage
and retrieval system, without permission in writing
from the publisher, except for brief quotations
in critical articles, books and reviews.

ISBN 13: 978-1-56184-547-6
ISBN 10: 1-56184-557-4

New Falcon Publications First Edition 2018
Second Printing 2022

The paper used in this publication meets the minimum requirements
of the American National Standard for Permanence of
Paper for Printed Library Materials Z39.48-1984

Printed in USA

NEW FALCON PUBLICATIONS
2046 Hillhurst Avenue
Los Angeles, CA 90027
www.newfalcon.com
email: info@newfalcon.com

CONTENTS

Introduction	vii
1. The Geomantic Symbols	1
2. Method	11
3. The Judge and Two Witnesses	27
4. The Question	31
5. The House	35
6. The Presiding Genius	39
7. Summary of Divining Process	49
8. An Example	71
9. Essential Dignities *From Vol. 5 of The Golden Dawn* *Complete System of Magic*	75

Introduction

In these days when the phrase 'extra-sensory perception' has become almost a by-word, our problem is not so much to discuss it, which is now relatively fruitless, but to develop it. It is really less a matter of development than of rendering explicit what is actually implicit. Just as everyone is moved by the spark of life without in most cases being aware of the direct mechanisms involved, so every man and woman possesses some latent capacity for extra-sensory perception. Some more, some less.

The major contribution of this book is not so much slanted in the direction of prediction of what is yet to come, but to facilitate the growth and expression of this inner psycho-spiritual ability. To this extent, any and all systems of divination may be considered useful. Amongst the more commonly used methods are the Tarot cards, astrology, palmistry, graphology, and many others. The method to be described here, geomancy, is favoured above all others because it is basically so simple to operate. One can use it quickly to obtain a simple 'yes' or 'no' answer. With sufficient practice, enough skill can be developed to provide considerable amplification of the first straight answer.

The more practical acquaintance one has with other divinatory systems, and the more one can bring that knowledge and experience to bear upon the geomantic reading, the more the primary simple reading can be extended. What is perhaps more important than most is an elementary knowledge of the basic principles of astrology. One does not need a profound working knowledge of astrology. But if there is some familiarity with the basic meanings of the planets, signs and houses, the mechanisms of geomancy become relatively easier to apply and understand.

The rationale of divination is admittedly obscure. A large tome could readily be written describing some of the ancient theories. This is not the place however to embark upon so ambitious an undertaking. A few lines of simple interpretation selected from the writings of Aleister Crowley and Carl G. Jung would not be amiss. With these basic ideas, the enterprising student can then propound his own theory to suit the psychological framework with which he is working.

In psychopathology it has already been securely established that unconscious psychic patterns influence and govern *all* conscious behaviour. The latter is motivated by what one psychological school has come to call 'complexes'–aggregates of mental contents, heavily charged with energy and feeling– or by what another school has termed 'archetypal images'. There is little need to hammer away at these basic facts; they have been too well and too long established.

It should become apparent then that the mechanisms of preparing the geomantic symbols to be used for the divination are almost completely under the control of these unconscious factors. We may assume, by the same token, that they have personalities of their own which, in geomancy, are called the governing Genii of the planets operating through the element of Earth.

Jung's definition of the Collective Unconscious, which is involved in these concepts, is so appropriate that I feel compelled to quote it as some length. In his book *Modern Man in Search of a Soul*, he wrote:

'It (the Unconscious) contains, besides an indeterminable number of subliminal perceptions, and immense fund of accumulated inheritance factors left by one generation of men after another, whose mere existence marks a step in the differentiation of the species. If it were permissible to personify the Unconscious, we might call it a collective human being combining the characteristics of both sexes, transcending youth and age, birth and death, and, from having at his command a human experience of one or two million years, almost immortal. If such a being existed, he would be exalted above all temporal change; the present would mean neither more nor less to him than any year in the one hundredth century before Christ; he would be a dreamer of age-old dreams, and, owing to his immeasurable prognosticator. He would have lived countless times over the life of the individual, of the family, tribe and people, and he would possess the living sense of the rhythms of growth, 'flowering and decay.'

It is from this basis that the dogmatic statement can be made that through the use of geomantic divination, this 'incomparable prognosticator' is permitted to operate and provide the answers to specific questions. Various aspects of this 'age-old dreamer of dreams' are invoked, as it were, by the geomantic technique, depending upon the type and nature of the matter enquired about.

Some of Crowley's thinking relative to divination is also particularly apt to our enquiry, and is therefore worth quoting.

'The theory of any process of divination may be stated in a few simple terms:

'1. We postulate the existence of intelligences, either within or without the diviner, of which he is not immediately conscious. (It does not matter he is not immediately conscious. (It does not matter to the theory whether the communicating spirit so called is an objective entity or a concealed portion of diviner's mind.) We assume that such intelligences are able to reply correctly–within limits–to the questions asked.

'2. We postulate that it is possible to construct a compendium of hieroglyphs sufficiently elastic in meaning to include every possible idea, and that one or more of these may always be taken to represent any idea. We assume that any of these hieroglyphics will be understood by the intelligences with whom we wish to communicate in the same sense as it is by ourselves...

'3. We postulate that the intelligences whom we wish to consult are willing, or may be compelled, to answer us truthfully.'

Chapter 1

THE GEOMANTIC SYMBOLS

There are only sixteen geomantic symbols. Each symbol consists of four lines, on each one there being either one dot or two dots. The single dot will hereafter be called odd or uneven, and the double dot will be called even. The sixteen figures are merely variations of the several ways in which one or two dots may be arranged in four lines. It is not wholly unlike the Yi King system in this respect where, from the simple Yin (broken) and Yang (unbroken) lines, sixty-four hexagrams are evolved, each with a specific meaning. Geomantic divination differs only in that the method of dealing with these sixteen symbols gives more complete and elaborate answers than does the Yi. The method of operation, however, is not too dissimilar: reliance upon the laws of chance, the geomantic intelligences, or the operation of the Unconscious psyche. For my purpose, they are equivalent terms.

These sixteen figures are attributed, first, to the four primitive elements of Earth, Air, Fire and Water. And then to the seven planets of the ancients, as well as to the twelve signs of the Zodiac. Only a few elementary descriptions need to be given here in reference to the signs and symbols. Experience will provide further elaboration.

1. *Puer*	*Mars*	*Fire*	*Aries*
x x x x x	♂	△	♈

Puer means in Latin 'a boy'; also 'yellow, beardless'. Its other symbols stamp it as having an energy significance. Aries is the first of the zodiacal signs, representing the beginning of the year, and thus the initiator of the events heralding growth and development. Since Aries is identified with the first house in geomancy, it also relates to the Self, and to the questioner himself.

The meaning of *Puer* varies as it is found in one house or another of the horoscopic map. The ancient description is 'Evil in most demands, excepting those relating to War or Love'.

2. *Amissio*	*Venus*	*Earth*	*Taurus*
x x x x x x	♀	▽	♉

Amissio means loss, even though the Venus attribution is considered astrologically to be one of the two benefits. To this extent, the geomantic differs from the standard astrological one. 'Good for loss of substance and sometimes for love, but *very bad* for gain.' For example, if a woman were seeking counsel as to whether she should divorce her husband, *Amissio* in the appropriate house would indicate a positive answer. On the other hand, so far as the possibility of alimony is concerned, the figure would be negative.

3. *Albus*   *Mercury*   *Air*   *Gemini*

```
x  x
x  x         ☿       △         ♊
   x
x  x
```

The Latin title means 'white' or 'white head', thus implying hoary wisdom, sagacity, clear thought–all mercurial definitions. Both the planet and the zodiacal sign rule the nervous system, stressing the fundamental idea of communication in all its manifold phases.

'Good for profit and for entering into a place or undertaking.' Gemini as the third house rules all that is within the immediate sphere of sensation. The third house mind does not make generalizations out of sense-experience; it does not form theories or doctrines. It is essentially 'practical'–sometimes superficial.

4. *Via*	*Populus*		*Moon*	*Water*	*Cancer*
x	x	x	☽	▽	♋
x	x	x			
x	x	x			
x	x	x			

This planet and sign has two geomantic figures attributed to it. *Via* means a 'street or a way'. *Populus* means a 'crowd' or a group'; perhaps also 'a congregation of people'. Both figures are essentially neutral, neither good nor bad in themselves; like the Moon and the element Water they merely reflect what provides their light or quality.

Via is said to be 'injurious to the goodness of other figures generally, but good for journeys and voyages'. *Populus* is 'sometimes good and sometimes bad; good with good, and evil with evil'.

The sign Cancer, as the fourth house, has a great deal to do with family, national and racial background, and the basis upon which the structure of life is built; security in other words. In so far as the Moon travels through all twelve signs in twenty-eight days, it is the symbol of change, inherent in the meaning of *Via*.

5. *Fortuna Major*		*Fortuna Minor*		*Sun*	*Fire*	*Leo*
x	x		x	☉	△	♌
x	x		x			
	x	x	x			
	x	x	x			

Like the preceding sign, two figures–the Greater and Lesser Fortunes–are attributed to the Sun, the source of all light and life and success. They represent good fortune obviously, interior and exterior aid, and are generally good figures for divination.

Leo is essentially egocentric, its native demanding a prominent place in the Sun: or better still the spotlight. The figure calls for fulfilment, suggesting also the possibilities of its achievement. Leo as the fifth house refers to any activity or process by which you externalize something of what you are within.

6. *Conjunctio*   *Mercury*   *Earth*   *Virgo*

```
x   x
  x           ☿       ▽       ♍
  x
x   x
```

This symbol means 'coming together, joining'. Its archaic definition is 'Good with good, or evil with evil. Recovery of things lost'.

Virgo is a cold, analytical sign, the practical side of things. Generally, she is neutral, neither good nor bad, but reflecting the over-all pattern. As the sixth house, Virgo represents the urge to do everything well; she is resourcefulness; one's attitude towards work.

7. *Puella*   *Venus*   *Air*   *Libra*

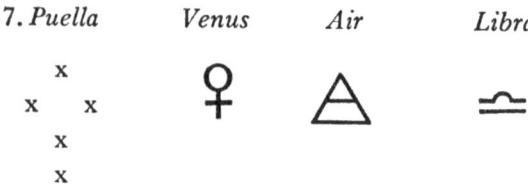

```
  x
x   x
  x
  x
```

Puella means 'a girl', or 'a pretty face'. It is pleasant but as a rule not too fortunate, any more than the mere possession of beauty itself is fortunate. The beautiful woman, though adored and loved for beauty is thereby harassed with manifold psychological problems that her plainer sister has never dreamed of. (In this connection, the essay on the beautiful woman in *The Problems of Everyday Life*, by Dr. Milton Sapirstein, is rewarding reading.) Charm rather than intellect or fiery passion produces the results obtained.

Puella is 'good in all demands, especially in those relating to women'. The sign-house represents any situation in which you are brought to face-to-face relationship on equal terms with anything external.

8. *Rubeus*   *Mars*   *Water*   *Scorpio*

```
x   x
  x
x   x
x   x
```

The Latin means 'red' or 'red-headed'. It refers to passion, fiery temper and vice, the traditional evil meanings relative to the sex-endowed sign of Scorpio. Most are exaggerated, over-simplifications of naïve ancient thinking: this is good, that is evil. Anyway, *Rubeus* represents force and power, destruction and evil outcomes. What direction this energy will take depends on the aspects to it in the chart. But all twelve readings of the symbol are evil, except in a few special instances where a show of aggression or eroticism is demanded: and then here the figure is most favourable.

9. *Acquisitio*　　　*Jupiter*　　　*Fire*　　　*Sagittarius*

```
x   x
  x           ♃      △      ♐
x   x
  x
```

Success, gain, good fortune–all traditional attributes of the major benefic Jupiter. In so far as Sagittarius and the ninth house are concerned, it also betokens travel, whether actually in the flesh moving from town to town or from country to country, or in the mind and spirit, as in philosophy and religion and law.

Acquisitio is 'generally good for profit and gain'. It is one of the most fortunate of all geomantic symbols, and should it occur as the significator it augurs well for the question.

10. *Carcer*   *Saturn*   *Earth*   *Capricorn*

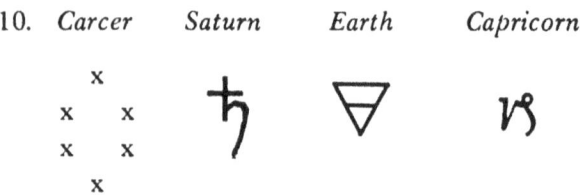

Carcer means 'prison', 'bound'. It reflects the outworn attitude relative to Saturn: evil, restriction, and the heavy hand of dismal fate. Tradition has it that if this particular symbol be found in the first house of the geomantic map, the divination is to be discontinued at once and the form wholly destroyed, with no further attempt being made to answer the same question for some hours.

Capricornians are supposed to be cold, methodical and practical–as well as altogether unemotional. Success is not forthcoming early in life, though the later years are brightened by a happier augury. 'Generally evil. Delay, binding, bars, restriction.'

11. *Tristitia*   *Saturn*   *Air*   *Aquarius*

Another heavy, cold Saturnine figure. It represents sadness, grief, condemnation. The geomantic interpretation does not closely adhere to the astrological description of Aquarius, though there are some vague parallels. It means unequivocally 'Evil in all things'. The only exceptions tradition makes are in those instances where the Saturnine attitude could be a thoroughgoing asset–where fortification might be wise, retrenching in business, for inheritance–or, strangely enough, even for having a gay old time which some of the mediaeval authorities labelled 'debauchery'.

12. *Laetitia*   *Jupiter*   *Water*   *Pisces*

```
  x
x   x       ♃     ▽     ♓
x   x
x   x
```

This is the exact opposite of the preceding figure. *Laetitia* means 'joy', and implies health and laughter. It is a high omen of good fortune, unlike the preceding figure which it counterbalances. 'Good for joy, present, or to come.' Here too, geomancy parts company with the conventional astrological interpretation of Pisces and the twelfth house to which it corresponds.

Two more figures, finally, need to be mentioned. They are named *Caput* and *Cauda Draconis*, the Head and Tail of the Dragon, supposed to be symbols of the Moon's northern and southern nodes. (Some authorities consider these two nodes to be symbolic equivalents of two other planets which the ancients knew about but kept wholly secret.)

Caput Draconis   *Cauda Draconis*

```
    X   X              X
      X                X
      X                X
      X              X   X
```

Caput Draconis–This is actually a good configuration, and means 'entrance, the inner threshold', the upper kingdom. 'Good with good, evil with evil. Gives a good issue for gain.'

Cauda Draconis–This is wholly an evil figure. It means 'the exit, the lower kingdom, the outer threshold'. It represents the harbinger of disaster. 'Good for evil, and for terminating affairs of any kind.' If this symbol occurs in the first house, the divination should be abandoned, and the forms destroyed.

Chapter 2

METHOD

To erect a geomantic chart is the essence of simplicity. The ancient method, which had its origins in the pre-civilized nomads of the desert, was to make some markings on sand or on the earth: thus geo and mantia, divination by earth. I have not found this primitive method too satisfactory, though I did experiment with it for a while. The particles of fine dry sand or earth are too readily disturbed by the wind, by random movements, and thus the chart itself is unstable and may be altered too quickly, even before it can be determined or interpreted.

A more modern and practical way is to employ a pad of paper and a good pencil. I suggest a very soft pencil be used or, better still, a contemporary broad-pointed Japanese marking pen, and that bright colours such as red or green be used instead of black. My reason for this recommendation is that thick red and green markings are less likely to be confused with some of the dark defects or spots to be found on many papers–and being brightly coloured stand out vividly from the background colour and can be counted more easily.

The pen or pencil is to be held firmly in the hand while one makes a line of dots quickly and mechanically, from left to right without counting. It is best to punctuate these dots as rapidly as possible in order to avoid the anticipation or temptation of counting them, and in so doing to control the outcome of the divination. I do not suggest passivity as in automatic writing, which I abhor, but a combination of muscular relaxation and mental alertness to prevent the ego from interfering with the process. The use of an invocation or a prayer for guidance–audible or inaudible–deflects the ego's attention from the mechanical process of making the dots, and thus permits the entire operation to be influenced by the Unconscious or the laws of chance. I will dilate on this topic later.

Sixteen rows of dots are to be made rapidly without thinking deliberately of the process. Only a little practice will render this task a simple one. The sixteen lines should be separated for convenience sake into four sections–as illustrated below–each section containing four lines. The illustration will hereafter be called Form No. 1.

Now look at the first row of dots. Count them carefully. It does not matter whether you count from the right moving to the left, or vice versa. My own procedure is to count from the left margin moving towards the right horizontal line where the boxes

. . . .	x x	
. . . .	x	
. . . .	x	
. . . .	x x	
	1	
. . . .	x x	
. . . .	x x	
. . . .	x	
. . . .	x x	
	2	
. . . .	x	
. . . .	x x	
. . . .	x x	
. . . .	x x	
	3	
. . . .	x	
. . . .	x	
. . . .	x	
. . . .	x	
	4	

N.B. The above four geomantic symbols have been selected at random, merely to pave the way for a technical description of how they are handled.

are. If the total on any one line comes to an odd number, you should enter a single dot in the space numbered 1. Should the total be an even number, then enter two dots.

Do the same thing with the second line of dots, adding them together to determine if the product is odd or even. Enter the results down in the space provided. Continue this process with all sixteen rows of dots. In this way, four basic or primary geomantic figures of four lines each will be produced. These four figures are called The Mothers.

Remember–and I must repeat this with emphasis–these sixteen lines of dots resulting in the first four geomantic symbols must be produced as mechanically or as unthinkingly as possible. This will permit their production to be under the aegis of the geomantic intelligences. No conscious selection of numbers of dots or the figure itself should be permitted. If it is permitted, the divination would be invalidated. The fact to be kept in mind is that the conscious ego is not 'the age-old dreamer of dreams' as Jung has stated it, nor an 'incomparable prognosticator of the future'.

All the other figures needed for the divination are to be drawn from the Four Mothers have recently been suggested by friends, methods which certainly emphasize strongly the chance factor, or manipulation by the Unconscious psyche. To this extent, they are much to be preferred. Before describing them, this admonition needs to be expressed. Whichever of the three methods you decide upon, he consistent in their use until mastery is acquired. Do not flit from one to another after you have made your first experimentations. Determine which one suits your personality first and then stick to that method.

The first of these new methods consists in the chance throwing of small pebbles. I understand it is similar to the process employed by Jung in connection with the Yi King. Obtain a small cereal or Japanese soup-bowl. Fill it with ordinary stone pebbles collected from a garden. If you have no garden or no pebbles, procure a number of multi-coloured or green pebbles from a 'rock-hound', or a store which caters for the amateur rock-collector. These stores are to be found in most large cities or adjacent thereto.

Then, with one hand, reach into the bowl and select a fistful, without counting the pebbles or prolonged fingering. Again, concentration on a symbol to be provided later, or repeating an invocatory sentence, will remove one's attention from what the hand is doing. Lift one's closed fistful of pebbles from the bowl and drop them on the table near the bowl. Count them. If the number of pebbles is, for example, ten– this is an even number, and so two dots be entered in the section numbered line No. 1, previously shown. In the event that the pebbles number thirteen, this is an odd number to be represented by a single dot in the section referred to.

As is quite evident, this is a very simple method– far simpler and easier, as well as more dependent on the laws of chance, than the former method of making a line of dots with a pencil.

The second of these newer methods is just as simple and uncomplicated. Obtain a small, dark green plastic tumbler, and two green dice. Green is selected as the natural colour for earth. Such tumblers and dice are often associated with children's games and games of chance. As such they are ideal for this purpose, and can be procured easily.

Shake the dice in the tumbler. While vibrating the invocation or thinking of the appropriate God-name or question, throw the dice on the table adjoining the pad. The same rule as above is to be followed. If the number on the dice add to an even total, such as 3 and 3 adding to 6, then enter two dots down in the appropriate section of the Form. If you get, however, 1 and 6, you have 7 as the total, which is an odd number requiring the recording of a single dot.

There will have to be sixteen separate throws of the pebbles or dice in order to get the sixteen lines which produce the Four Mothers. These I have arbitrarily numbered from 1-4 on the Form, as a description of their management is thus rendered more simple.

Now to the other figures. The next four figures, numbered on the Form from 5-8 inclusive, are called the Four Daughters. They are directly derived from the preceding four Figures which, let us assume, we have already obtained.

The method is the essence of simplicity itself. The first line of Figure 1 is transferred to the first line of section 5, thus becoming the first line of the fifth geomantic figure. The first line of Figure 2 becomes the second line of No. 5. The first line of Figure 4 becomes the fourth line of Figure 5. Thus:

```
x   x
x   x           Fortuna Major
  x
  x
```

A similar procedure is to be followed in obtaining the sixth geomantic figure:

The 2nd line of Figure 1 becomes the 1st line of Figure No. 6
The 2nd line of Figure 2 becomes the 2nd line of Figure No. 6
The 2nd line of Figure 3 becomes the 3rd line of Figure No. 6
The 2nd line of Figure 4 becomes the 4th line of Figure No. 6

```
  x
x   x           Carcer
x   x
  x
```

Similarly with the 7th figure:

The 3rd line of Figure 1 becomes the 1st line of Figure No. 7
The 3rd line of Figure 2 becomes the 2nd line of Figure No. 7
The 3rd line of Figure 3 becomes the 3rd line of Figure No. 7
The 3rd line of Figure 4 becomes the 4th line of Figure No. 7

Thus:

```
    x
    x              Puer
 x     x
    x
```

And so with the 8th Figure:

The 4th line of Figure 1 becomes the 1st line of Figure No. 8
The 4th line of Figure 2 becomes the 2nd line of Figure No. 8
The 4th line of Figure 3 becomes the 3rd line of Figure No. 8
The 4th line of Figure 4 becomes the 4th line of Figure No. 8

Thus:

```
 x   x
 x   x          Tristitia
 x   x
    x
```

And in this way the second set of Figures or the Four Daughters are evolved out of the Four Mothers, the first set of geomantic figures. Enter these in the second column on Form No. 1 in the appropriately marked spaces. Tradition ascribe anatomical names to these lines or parts, such as: 1. Head; 2. Neck; 3. Body; 4. Feet. I rarely use these terms nowadays, but they may just as well be mentioned for the sake of completeness.

The third set of geomantic figures are called the Four Nephews. They are evolved from the preceding eight figures in a rather different but still simple way. The first two Mothers are added together to produce the first Nephew or Figure 9 on the Form. If the addition produces even numbers, two dots are recorded; if odd, then single dots are entered down. For example:

Figure 1   *Figure 2*

  X   X   X   X
    X   X   X
  X   +   X
  X   X   X   X

If line 1 of each of these two figures is added together you get four, an even number, to be represented in the appropriate space by two dots.

Line 2 of both figures add to 3, an odd number, and so represented by one dot.

Line 3 of both figures add to 2, which is an even number represented by two dots.

Line 4 of both figures add to 4, an even number—thus two dots. These four lines are therefore:

  X   X
    X   *Rubeus*
  X   X
  X   X

The second Nephew or Figure 10 is produced by joining together the 3rd and 4th Mothers in this way:

```
Figure 3        Figure 4        Figure 10
   x               x             x   x
 x   x             x               x         Caput
 x   x      +      x      =        x        Draconis
 x   x             x               x
```

The third Nephew or Figure 11 is produced by adding together the first two Daughters, using precisely the same technique as was used previously with the Mothers, viz:

```
Figure 5        Figure 6        Figure 11
 x   x             x               x
 x   x           x   x           x   x      Amissio
   x      +      x   x     =       x
   x               x             x   x
```

The fourth Nephew or Figure 12 is produced similarly:

```
Figure 7        Figure 8        Figure 12
   x             x   x             x
   x             x   x             x        Fortuna
 x   x    +      x   x     =     x   x       Minor
   x               x             x   x
```

The completed Form with all twelve geomantic figures duly entered in their proper positions will now look like this:

Line No.	1.	x x	x x	x x
	2.	x	x x	x
	3.	x	x	x x
	4.	x x	x	x x
		1	5	9
Line No.	5.	x x	x	x x
	6.	x x	x x	x
	7.	x	x x	x
	8.	x x	x	x
		2	6	10
Line No.	9.	x	x	x
	10.	x x	x	x x x
	11.	x x	x x	x x
	12.	x x	x	
		3	7	11
Line No.	13.	x	x x	x
	14.	x	x x	x
	15.	x	x x	x x
	16.	x	x	x x
		4	8	12

L.W.	R.W.	Judge

From this completed Form No. 1, the twelve major figures are then transferred to Form No. 2, which is really a mediaeval form of horoscopal chart (which today is circular):

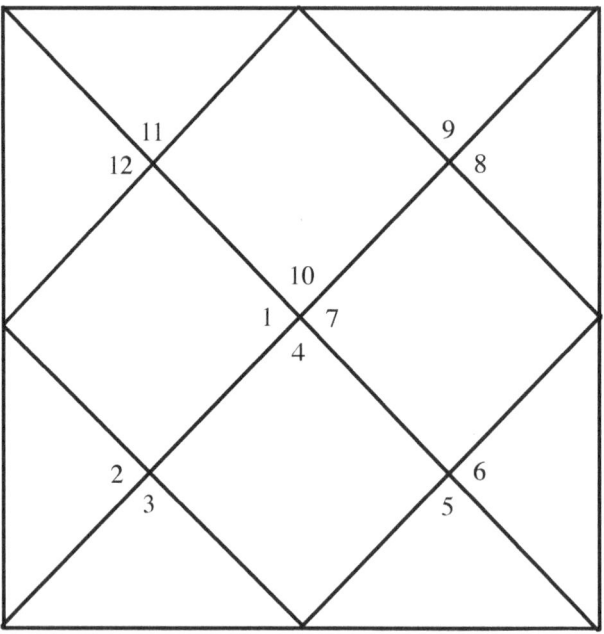

The numbers in the above form represent the twelve astrological houses. Their meanings can be given briefly as follows:

1. (Also called the Ascendant.) Life, health, querent, etc.
2. Money, property, personal worth, possessions.
3. Brothers, sisters, news, short journeys, all communications.
4. Father, landed property, inheritance, the grave. Also the end of the matter enquired about.
5. Children, pleasure, love, feasts, speculation, creativity.
6. Servants, sickness and health, uncles and aunts, small animals.
7. Marriage, husband or wife. Partnerships, contracts and associations, public enemies, lawsuits.
8. Death, wills, legacies. Pain, anxiety. Estate of deceased.
9. Long journeys, voyages. Science, religion, art. Visions and divinations.
10. Mother, rank and honour, trade or profession. Authority, employment, and worldly position generally.
11. Friends, hopes and wishes.
12. Sorrows, fears, punishments, enemies in secret, institutions, unseen dangers, restriction, hospitals or prisons.

It would be useful for the student to memorize this table of house-meanings. The business of interpretation will be rendered relatively painless if these are at the tip of his tongue.

The order in which figures from Form No. 1 are transferred to the horoscope Form No. 2 is as follows:

Geomantic Figure No. 1 is placed in the 10th house on Form No. 2
Geomantic Figure No. 5 is placed in the 11th house on Form No. 2
Geomantic Figure No. 9 is placed in the 12th house on Form No. 2
Geomantic Figure No. 2 is placed in the 1st house on Form No. 2
Geomantic Figure No. 6 is placed in the 2nd house on Form No. 2
Geomantic Figure No. 10 is placed in the 3rd house on Form No. 2
Geomantic Figure No. 3 is placed in the 4th house on Form No. 2
Geomantic Figure No. 7 is placed in the 5th house on Form No. 2
Geomantic Figure No. 11 is placed in the 6th house on Form No. 2
Geomantic Figure No. 4 is placed in the 7th house on Form No. 2
Geomantic Figure No. 8 is placed in the 8th house on Form No. 2
Geomantic Figure No. 12 is placed in the 9th house on Form No. 2

This sounds far more complicated than it really is. Keep referring to the two charts, and even make copies of them on loose leaf paper so that you have them in front of you when using the above tabulation. Only a couple of attempts to put the right figures on the map in the correct order will clear up the apparent difficulty once and for all.

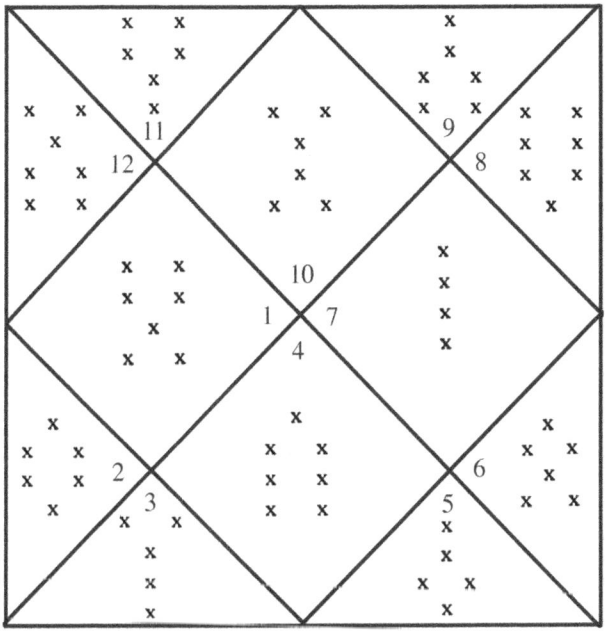

Trines
Squares
Sextiles
Opposition
4th House:
Interpretation:

Chapter 3

THE JUDGE AND TWO WITNESSES

Just prior to beginning interpretation, right after the geomantic figures have been correctly set up on the chart, it may be a considerable advantage to obtain three additional geomantic figures which will enable one to arrive at a quicker but definite answer. It will be from what these three figures imply, that one will be able to make a 'yes' or 'no' judgment.

Take the 9th and 10th Geomantic figure on Form No. 1–these are the first two Nephews, the third derivative set of symbols–and add them together in the manner to which, by now, you are well accustomed.

```
Figure 9      Figure 10    Left Witness
  x   x        x   x         x   x
    x             x           x   x      Fortuna
  x   x           x             x        Major
  x   x           x             x
         +              =
```

Then take the 11th and 12th figures, the last two Nephews, from From No. 1, and add them together, thus:

```
Figure 11   Figure 12    Right Witness
    x            x             x   x
  x   x          x               x
    x     +    x   x    =        x         Conjunctio
  x   x      x   x             x   x
```

The final figure called the Judge is then constructed out of the addition of both the Right and Left Witnesses:

```
Left Witness    Right Witness    Judge
  x   x            x   x         x   x
  x   x              x             x
    x       +        x     =     x   x     Acquisitio
    x              x   x           x
```

A reading can then be made entirely from these three figures. A 'yes' or 'no' answer is immediately available. If my question had been 'Should I buy a home now?' The answer is yes. *Acquisitio* is a favourable figure, but one which requires immediate action.

For the sake of completeness, the Judge can be compared to the Significator. The latter is the geomantic figure in the specific House of the particular matter enquired about in the question or divination. Should the meaning still remain obscure, their points may be added together in the now conventional way to yield a new figure called the Reconciler. Obviously, as the name implies, this figure reconciles the meanings of both the Judge and the Significator.

The reading made from the Judge and Two Witnesses can interpreted in terms of a beginning middle and end. The Left Witness could represent the beginning of the matter; the Right Witness the way in which it progresses, and the Judge indicating the final disposition of the matter. In this instance, the figure of *Fortuna Major* indicates that whatever the question may have been, the beginning will be altogether satisfactory. The Right Witness is a neutral figure more or less, but since the other witness is a good symbol, as is the last figure or Judge, it takes on a benign significance. The Judge is *Acquisitio*, which on the whole is benefic.

Space for the two Witnesses and the Judge should be marked at the bottom of Form No. 1.

PLANET:
GENIUS:

| L.W. | R.W. | Judge |

Chapter 4

THE QUESTION

It was once written by Aleister Crowley in his book *Magick* that the intelligences used in geomancy–the earth elementals or gnomes–are not too reliable, or that their *type* of intelligence is not of the highest. Therefore great care has to be exercised lest they be given an opportunity to deceive, or lest confusion and misunderstanding arise because the wording of the question has been carelessly considered. Whether or not one agrees with the above, there should be no disagreement concerning the absolute necessity of employing a clearly worded question. There must be no usage of a query in which there is a choice of two directions, or things, such as 'Should I do this or that?' Obviously this will result only in a confused answer, or an answer which the enquirer secretly wishes to obtain. Nor should the question be phrased in the form of a moral judgment: 'Should I abscond with the bank's assets?' Morality is essentially a human acquisition. Conscience is unknown to the earth elementals. To confront them with this factor is to force them to deal with variable human factors which are entirely foreign to their structure.

If I asked the question for example, 'Will this book be successful?' one becomes aware of the fact that many obscure issues are raised. Since there is no specificity for the gnomes to work with, no specific answer can be expected. What book is referred to? Name is clearly, if you would avoid confusion. The title then, *A Practical Guide to Geomantic Divination*, should be made part of the question.

Again, what is meant by the word 'successful'? And for whom? Does it mean book sales going into hundreds of thousands of copies? Hardbacked or paperbacked? Does 'success' raise the issue of money? Will I make any money out of it? Does successful mean that it will please me? Or the publisher? Or does it convey the idea that it will really and truly succeed in instructing the interested segment of the public in the art of geomantic divination?

The question and all its implications must be clearly thought out, as you can perceive, and phrased properly and accurately before the divining process really begins. There must be absolutely no room for ambiguity. The matter must be clearly defined, and then properly worded. In that case, the answer will be clearly given. One must not assume that the 'age-old dreamer of dreams' is omniscient, even if he is an 'incomparable prognosticator' of future events.

Here are some examples of simple questions based upon those given many years ago by Dr. Franz Hartmann. Direct answers of 'yes' or 'no' can be obtained to these and other questions.

1. Will the person enquired about have a long life?
2. Will he become rich?
3. Will the proposed undertaking be successful?
4. How will the undertaking end?
5. Is the expected child a boy or a girl?
6. Are the servants honest?
7. Will the patient recover soon?
8. Will the lover succeed in getting his girl (or vice versa)?
9. Will the inheritance be obtained?
10. Will the lawsuit come to a satisfactory end for me?
11. Will I (or he) obtain the desired position?
12. What kind of death may be expected?
13. Will the expected letters arrive?
14. Will the voyage be fortunate?
15. Will good news arrive?
16. Will the adversary be conquered?

Even these should be edited more closely to avoid even the slightest taint of ambiguity.

Chapter 5

THE HOUSE

Once the precise wording of the question has been settled, and one is satisfied that it is clear and concise, write it down at the top of the form. Then consult the list of houses and their definitions. Decide upon the house and their definitions. Decide upon the house on the chart where on should look for the Significator after all the figures have been duly entered.

For example, consider the question 'Will *A Practical Guide to Geomantic Divination* be published?' The ninth house, we will discover, deals with the topic of divination. The third house properly deals with its writing, while the seventh house should relate to the contract with the publisher if and when the book has been accepted for publication. The second house refers to any possible income or royalties from the sale of the book.

But it is the ninth house that we will consider as important as the house of signification. The geomantic figure found in that house will be considered as the Significator. This too should be written down at the top of the Form No. 1. This procedure helps to give order and form to one's mind, direction to the elementals, and a clear answer to the divination.

The next matter to be considered is the planetary rulership. Here follows a list of the planetary meanings:

1. *Saturn*. Older people and old plans. Debts and their repayment. Agriculture, real estate. Death and wills. Stability and inertia. Time, patience, and testing.
2. *Jupiter*. Abundance, plenty, growth, expansion, generosity. Spirituality, visions, dreams, long journeys. Bankers, creditors, debtors, gambling. Success.
3. *Mars*. Energy, haste, anger. Construction or destruction, according to context and application. Danger, accidents, surgery, vitality, and magnetism.
4. *Sun*. Superiors, employers, executives, officials. Power and success. Life, money, growth of all kinds. Illumination, imagination, mental power and creativity. Health.
5. *Venus*. Social affairs, affections and emotions, women, younger people. All pleasures, including the arts: music, beauty, extravagance, luxury and self-indulgence.
6. *Mercury*. Business matters. Writing, contracts, judgment, and short travels. Buying, selling, bargaining. Neighbours,

giving and obtaining information. Literary capabilities and intellectual friends. Books, papers, communications, publications.

7. *Moon*. General public, women. Sense reactions. Short journeys and removals. Changes and fluctuations. The personality.

What planet would publication come under? Generally speaking, both the writing and publication are considered forms of communication, which are thus ruled by the planet Mercury. Put this down on the form at the top of the page. All is now in order.

Note the variations possible. Had the question related to success, not merely publication, the planetary ruler would have been either Jupiter or the Sun. Were the question '*Will A Practical Guide to Geomantic Divination* endure for a long time?' Its planetary rulership would have been Saturn. If one had asked whether women rather than men would become attracted to the book, Venus would have had to be the planetary ruler.

Enough has been said on this topic to indicate that care, too, has to be exercised on this matter just as it has with regard to the formulation of the question itself.

Chapter 6

THE PRESIDING GENIUS

All previous exoteric works dealing with geomancy are defective in this one particular area at least, the omission of that procedure which is an initiated technique.

Geomancy is divination through the element Earth. In one of the rituals of the Hermetic Order of the Golden Dawn the initiate is sworn to invoke, in his workings, the highest name of God that he knows. In this way, whatever he does will come under the guidance and benediction of the highest spiritual force that he knows. Thus the ruler of the element of Earth has to be magically invoked so that it may truly govern this work of prognostication. It comprises three separate gestures:

1. The invocation of the God-name ruling the element Earth.
2. Tracing the appropriate invoking Earth Pentagram.
3. Summoning the appropriate presiding Genius which rules over the question at hand.

In the Qabalah, which is the occult philosophy upon which this initiated interpretation of geomancy is predicted, the element of Earth is placed under the divine aegis of that aspect of God attributed to Malkuth, the tenth Sephirah on the Tree of Life. The divine name is *Adonai ha-Aretz*–meaning 'The Lord of the Earth'. (Its pronunciation can be described thus: Ah-doh-nye hah-Ah-retz.) When opening the divinatory process by the method to be described, this name should be softly intoned or vibrated so that one's mind may be exalted above temporal and mundane preoccupations. In this way it is tuned in, as it were, to the Highest.

Furthermore, the element of Earth is attributed to one of the five points of the Pentagram, the geometrical figure always used in the sanctuary of the Gnosis to invoke all elements. With the Pentagram standing up on the two lower angles, the topmost point at the summit, then the lower left point represents the Earth angle. The fundamental rule of invocation is 'move towards the angle to invoke. Move away from the appropriate angle to banish'.

Since we wish to invoke the element of Earth, we must start therefore at the topmost single point and move downwards to the left, viz:

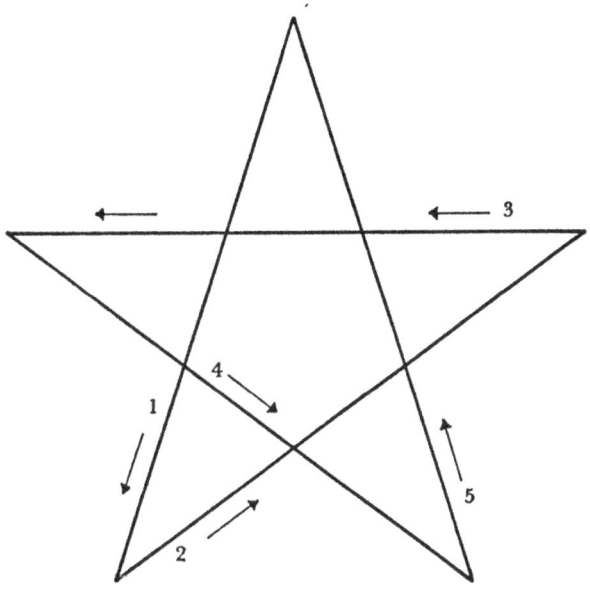

The weapon employed for invoking is the coloured pen or pencil used to record the geomantic symbols as already described. First of all, however, take the small plastic cup or tumbler employed to shake the dice, and invert it near the top of Form No. 1. Trace a circle with your pen or pencil around the circumference of the cup, touching the paper. Remove the cup, and you will find you have drawn a near perfect circle.

Now very carefully mark on the circumference of this circle five points corresponding to the points of the pentagram. You can either work this out

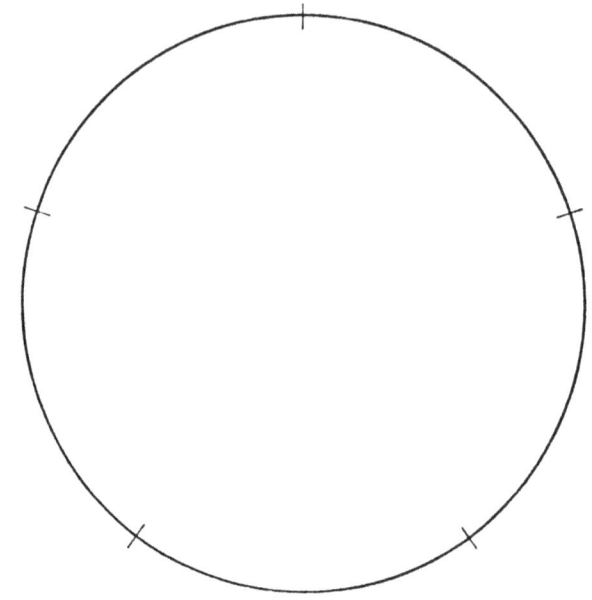

mathematically, or with the aid of a compass–or else guess as best as you can. This circle marked by five points will ensure that while tracing the invoking Earth Pentagram, there will be no clumsy groping that might result in the drawing of a malformed geometrical figure. While drawing this figure from the uppermost pint down to the lowermost left angle, and then completing the figure, the divine name already given should be audibly or subvocally vibrated, as many times as you feel may be necessary.

One more feature remains to be stated, and this is most important, differentiating the initiated approach from the profane. To every planetary force in geomancy, there is attributed a Genius presiding over all matters covered by the definitions of that force. This Genius is an Earth elemental of considerable stature. His name is given in the following table, together with his sigil, a traditional word that merely means a signature. This sigil should be very deliberately and carefully drawn in the centre of the Pentagram which has been traced. It should be visualized as clearly as is possible, while vibrating his name several times, either vocally or mentally. This places the whole divinitory process under divine guidance, and opens up specific pathways to the Unconscious area which can act to provide an answer to the question.

These basic facts must now be drawn together and amalgamated to provide for a clear and perfect divination. The Form No. 1 which we are using for the purpose may now be finally elaborated to cover each one of these several points which have been described.

QUESTION:
HOUSE:

PLANET:
GENIUS:

| L.W. | R.W. | JUDGE |

FORM No. 1

This completes the purely mechanical discussion of forming and erecting the geomantic chart. All phases of the process should be thoroughly studied, the essentials memorized, and practised sufficiently afterwards, so that the figures can be made literally without effort. Doing half a dozen divinations is frankly all that is required to achieve this end easily.

Many to whom I have taught the method in recent years have really experienced little or no difficulty at all. A lawyer friend, to whom I demonstrated the art within the past six months, became relatively expert in one afternoon after having erected less than half a dozen charts.

The textbook description, I must admit, does sound most complicated. In practice, however, it is thoroughly simple. The moral involved here is do not be content merely to read the description given. Practise simultaneously. The ability to divine and predict successfully will be its own reward, and provide the needed stimulus to experiment still further.

GEOMANTIC ATTRIBUTIONS

Sigil of Ruler	Name of Ruler	Planet which rules Answer	Sign of Zodiac	Element	Geomantic Figure	Geomantic Name and Meaning of Figure
♌︎	Bartzabel	Mars ♂	Aries ♈	Fire	:· ·: ··	PUER (a boy, yellow, beardless)
♉︎	Kedemel	Venus ♀	Taurus ♉	Earth	·· :· ·: ··	AMISSIO (loss, comprehended without)
☿	Taphthartharath	Mercury ☿	Gemini ♊	Air	·· ·· :· ··	ALBUS (white, fair)
♋︎	Chasmodai	Luna ☽	Cancer ♋	Water	:: :: :: ::	POPULUS (people, congregation)
♌︎	Sorath	Sol ☉	Leo ♌	Fire	·: ·: :· :·	FORTUNA MAJOR (greater fortune and aid; safeguard, entering)
☿	Taphthartharath	Mercury ☿	Virgo ♍	Earth	:· ·: ·: ·:	CONJUNCTIO (assembly, conjunction)
♉︎	Kedemel	Venus ♀	Libra ♎	Air	·: ·: ·: ··	PUELLA (a girl, beautiful)
♌︎	Bartzabel	Mars ♂	Scorpio ♏	Water	·: ·: ·: ·:	RUBEUS (red)

Sigil of Ruler	Name of Ruler	Planet which rules Answer	Sign of Zodiac	Element	Geomantic Figure	Name and Meaning of Figure
↙	Hismael	Jupiter ♃	Sagittarius ♐	Fire	· · · · · ·	ACQUISITIO (obtaining, comprehended within)
◊	Zazel	Saturn ♄	Capricorn ♑	Earth	· · · · · ·	CARCER (a prison, bound)
◊	Zazel	Saturn ♄	Aquarius ♒	Air	· · · · · · · · · ·	TRISTITIA (sadness, damned, cross)
↙	Hismael	Jupiter ♃	Pisces ♓	Water	· · · · · · · ·	LAETITIA (joy, laughing, healthy, bearded)
◊ ♌	Zazel and Bartzabel	Saturn and Mars ♂	Cauda Draconis ☋	Fire	· · · · · · · ·	CAUDA (the lower DRACONIS threshold, going out)
☽ ℞	Hismael and Kedemel	Venus and ♀ Jupiter ♃	Caput Draconis ☊	Earth	· · · · · · · ·	CAPUT DRACONIS (heart, upper threshold, entering)
	Sorath	Sol ☉	Leo ♌	Fire	· · · · · · ·	FORTUNA MINOR (lesser fortune and aid; safeguard, going out)
♋	Chasmodai	Luna ☽	Cancer ♋	Water	· · · ·	VIA (way, journey)

Chapter 7

SUMMARY OF DIVINING PROCESS

1. Determine the question to be asked, and word it clearly.
2. Consider what house on the chart should be involved.
3. What planetary force would govern the nature of the question.
4. Then decide upon the Genius to be invoked.
5. Write the above on the top of the blank to be used.
6. Mark the five points around the circumference of the circle which has been traced with the aid of the plastic tumble.
7. While making the invoking Pentagram, vibrate the divine name ruling the element Earth.
8. Very carefully, draw within the centre of the Pentagram the sigil of the Genius. Vibrate his name several times.
9. If you proceed by tracing the dots, concentrate on the question and repeat it many times to distract the mind from counting.

10. If you use the pebbles or dice, similarly verbalize the question.
11. Count sixteen lines of dots, or throw the pebbles or dice sixteen times. The mechanical part of the divination is over.
12. Construct the first four figures, and derive from them the remaining eight.
13. Construct the Witnesses and Judge.
14. Enter the twelve geomantic figures on the Chart.
15. If need be, make a Reconciler.

The mechanical part of obtaining the necessary geomantic symbols completed, it remains only to interpret what you have entered on Form No. 2. Some imagination and ingenuity needs to be employed, but the following tables of general interpretation should take the slack out of the first several attempts to divine. As one gains experience, enough confidence with be created to permit the intuition to operate, or to say what comes to mind spontaneously, without critical interference from the ego. Gradually, as time goes on, the intuition or inner psychic sense will become stronger, clearer and of course more reliable. Geomantic divination as a process is a good psychological corrective for excessive intellectually, or for uncontrolled flights of fantasy based on romantic reading. A little practice goes a long way.

The proof of geomantic divination is success in prediction: in the business of sharpening your wits or intuitive processes.

A systematic plan should be evolved which one follows consistently in the art of interpretation. The geomantic figure in the important house of the question asked–the Significator–should be thoroughly observed and studied. It should then be compared to the Judge by the methods already described to produce another figure called the Reconciler. This too should be studied in the light of the question asked, and the interpretations given on the charts that follow.

The close relationship between astrology and geomancy now becomes apparent. One searches for the aspects between the Significator and the other figures in the chart. There are trines, squares, sextiles and oppositions to be considered, as in astrology. I have constructed some simple rules to help establish these aspects.

1. For the trine △ aspect, count five houses from and including the Significator, in both directions, clockwise and the reverse. Thus, there are two trines. The trine in the clockwise direction, called dexter, is stronger in effect than the trine moving in the other direction. Consider the meaning of what houses these figures fall in and reflect that the trine is a favourable aspect, increasing good and minimizing the adverse.

2. For the Square ☐ aspect, count four houses from and including the Significator in both directions. Thus there are two squares. Usually it is a bad aspect, representing a challenge of some sort, an obstacle that may or may not be overcome successfully. This depends on the geomantic figures found in those houses.

3. For the Sextile ✶ aspect, count three houses from and including the Significator in both directions. Thus there are two sextiles, mildly beneficent aspects.

4. The Opposition ☍ is of course directly opposite to the Significator, 180° away–or a count of seven houses from and including the Significator. It indicates the nature and meaning of the chief difficulties to be expected.

These aspects should be entered down on Form No. 2 beneath the chart, in the lines so marked. Again, in this way one tends to organize and render methodical the interpretations of the geomantic symbols. Use the interpretation charts frequently, as often as may be required, meditating on the meaning of the change of interpretation in this house or another. Gradually the chief meanings will become impressed on the memory to be used as and when required.

Then a review should be made. A little story should be woven, using vividly the imaginative faculty, incorporating all these multiple factors. One could content oneself easily with a 'yes' or 'no' answer, or 'good' or 'bad'. Or one can make the reading as detailed and meticulous as one can imagine, very full and informative.

One last point needs to be mentioned. After having examined all the figures and their many aspects, and reached a mature judgment concerning the question, look to the fourth house. It relates to 'the end of the matter', the final disposition of the question asked. It summates all the previously gathered data. The beginning may be poor, come to a fairly good climax, but how ultimately will it end? This is answered by the figure in the fourth house. Examining this, and incorporating its findings into the final interpretation, should never be omitted.

TABLES OF GENERAL INTERPRETATION

ACQUISITIO

Generally good for profit and gain.

Ascendant	Happy, success in all things.
Second House	Very prosperous.
Third House	Favour and riches.
Fourth House	Good fortune and success.
Fifth House	Good success.
Sixth House	Good–especially if it agrees with the 5th.
Seventh House	Reasonably good.
Eighth House	Rather good, but not very. The sick shall die.
Ninth House	Good in all demands.
Tenth House	Good in suits. Very prosperous.
Eleventh House	Good in all.
Twelfth House	Evil, pain and loss.

AMISSIO

Good for loss of substance and sometimes for love; but *very bad* for gain.

Ascendant	Ill in all things but for prisoners.
Second House	Very ill for money, but good for love.
Third House	Ill end–except for quarrels.
Fourth House	Ill in all.
Fifth House	Evil except for agriculture.
Sixth House	Rather evil for love.
Seventh House	Very good for love, otherwise evil.
Eighth House	Excellent in all questions.
Ninth House	Evil in all things.
Tenth House	Evil except for favour with women.
Eleventh House	Good for love, otherwise bad.
Twelfth House	Evil in all things.

FORTUNA MAJOR

Good for gain in all things where a person has hopes to win.

Ascendant	Good save in secrecy.
Second House	Good except in sad things.
Third House	Good in all.
Fourth House	Good in all, but melancholy.
Fifth House	Very good in all things.
Sixth House	Very good except for debauchery.
Seventh House	Good in all.
Eighth House	Moderately good.
Ninth House	Very good.
Tenth House	Exceedingly good. Go to superiors.
Eleventh House	Very good.
Twelfth House	Good in all.

FORTUNA MINOR

Good in any matter in which a person wishes to proceed quickly.

Ascendant	Speed in victory and in love, but choleric.
Second House	Very good.
Third House	Good–but wrathful.
Fourth House	Haste; rather evil except for peace.
Fifth House	Good in all things.
Sixth House	Medium in all.
Seventh House	Evil except for war or love.
Eighth House	Evil generally.
Ninth House	Good, but choleric.
Tenth House	Good, except for peace.
Eleventh House	Good, especially for love.
Twelfth House	Good, except for alteration, or for suing another.

LAETITIA

Good for joy, present or to come.

Ascendant	Good, except in war.
Second House	Sickly.
Third House	Ill.
Fourth House	Mainly good.
Fifth House	Excellently good.
Sixth House	Evil generally.
Seventh House	Indifferent.
Eighth House	Evil, generally.
Ninth House	Very good.
Tenth House	Good, rather in war than in peace.
Eleventh House	Good in all.
Twelfth House	Evil generally.

TRISTITIA

Evil in almost all things.

Ascendant	Medium, but good for treasure and fortifying.
Second House	Medium, but good to fortify.
Third House	Evil in all.
Fourth House	Evil in all.
Fifth House	Very evil.
Sixth House	Evil, except for debauchery.
Seventh House	Evil for inheritance and magic only.
Eighth House	Evil, but in secrecy good.
Ninth House	Evil except for magic.
Tenth House	Evil except for fortifications.
Eleventh House	Evil in all.
Twelfth House	Evil, but good for magic and treasure.

PUELLA

Good in all demands, especially in those relating to women.

Ascendant	Good except in war.
Second House	Very good.
Third House	Good.
Fourth House	Indifferent.
Fifth House	Very good, but notice the aspects.
Sixth House	Good, but especially so for debauchery.
Seventh House	Good except for war.
Eighth House	Good.
Ninth House	Good for music. Otherwise only medium.
Tenth House	Good for peace.
Eleventh House	Good, and love of ladies.
Twelfth House	Good in all.

PUER

Evil in most demands, except in those relating to war or love.

Ascendant	Indifferent. Best in war.
Second House	Good, but with trouble.
Third House	Good fortune.
Fourth House	Evil, except in war and love.
Fifth House	Medium good.
Sixth House	Medium.
Seventh House	Evil, save for war.
Eighth House	Evil, save for love.
Ninth House	Evil except for war.
Tenth House	Rather evil. But good for love and war. Most other things medium.
Eleventh House	Medium; good favour.
Twelfth House	Very good in all.

RUBEUS

Evil in all that is good and good in all that is evil.

Ascendant	Destroy the figure if it falls here! It makes the judgment worthless.
Second House	Evil in all demands.
Third House	Evil except to let blood.
Fourth House	Evil except in war and fire.
Fifth House	Evil save for love, and sowing seed.
Sixth House	Evil except for blood-letting.
Seventh House	Evil except for war and fire.
Eighth House	Evil.
Ninth House	Very evil.
Tenth House	Dissolute. Love, fire.
Eleventh House	Evil, except to let blood.
Twelfth House	Evil in all things.

ALBUS

Good for profit and for entering into a place or undertaking.

Ascendant	Good for marriage. Mercurial. Peace.
Second House	Good in all.
Third House	Very good.
Fourth House	Very good except in war.
Fifth House	Good.
Sixth House	Good in all things.
Seventh House	Good except for war.
Eighth House	Good.
Ninth House	A messenger brings a letter.
Tenth House	Excellent in all.
Eleventh House	Very good.
Twelfth House	Marvelously good.

CONJUNCTIO

Good with good, or evil with evil. Recovery of things lost.

Ascendant	Good with good, evil with evil.
Second House	Commonly good.
Third House	Good fortune.
Fourth House	Good save for health; see the 8th.
Fifth House	Medium.
Sixth House	Good for immorality only.
Seventh House	Rather good.
Eighth House	Evil; death.
Ninth House	Medium good.
Tenth House	For love, good. For sickness, evil.
Eleventh House	Good in all.
Twelfth House	Medium. Bad for prisoners.

CARCER

Generally evil. Delay, binding, bar, restriction.

Ascendant	Evil except to fortify a place.
Second House	Good in Saturnine questions; else evil.
Third House	Evil.
Fourth House	Good only for melancholy.
Fifth House	Receive a letter within three days.
Sixth House	Very evil.
Seventh House	Evil.
Eighth House	Very evil.
Ninth House	Evil in all.
Tenth House	Evil save for hidden treasure.
Eleventh House	Much anxiety.
Twelfth House	Rather good.

CAPUT DRACONIS

Good with good; evil with evil. Gives a good issue for gain.

Ascendant	Good in all things.
Second House	Good.
Third House	Very good.
Fourth House	Good save in war.
Fifth House	Very good.
Sixth House	Good for immorality only.
Seventh House	Good especially for peace.
Eighth House	Good.
Ninth House	Very good.
Tenth House	Good in all.
Eleventh House	Good for the church and ecclesiastical gain.
Twelfth House	Not very good.

CAUDA DRACONIS

Good with evil, and evil with good. Good for loss, and for passing out of an affair.

Ascendant	Destroy figure if it falls here! Makes judgment worthless.
Second House	Very evil.
Third House	Evil in all.
Fourth House	Good especially for conclusion of the matter.
Fifth House	Very evil.
Sixth House	Rather good.
Seventh House	Evil, war, and fire.
Eighth House	No good, except for magic.
Ninth House	Good for science only. Bad for journeys. Robbery.
Tenth House	Evil save in works of fire.
Eleventh House	Evil save for favours.
Twelfth House	Rather good.

VIA

Injurious to the goodness of other figures generally, but good for journeys and voyages.

Ascendant	Evil except for prison.
Second House	Indifferent.
Third House	Very good in all.
Fourth House	Good in all save love.
Fifth House	Voyages good.
Sixth House	Evil.
Seventh House	Rather good, especially for voyages.
Eighth House	Evil.
Ninth House	Indifferent. Good for journeys.
Tenth House	Good.
Eleventh House	Very good.
Twelfth House	Excellent.

POPULUS

Sometimes good and sometimes bad; good with good, and evil with evil.

Ascendant	Good for marriage.
Second House	Medium good.
Third House	Rather good than bad.
Fourth House	Good in all but love.
Fifth House	Good in most things.
Sixth House	Good.
Seventh House	In war good, else medium.
Eighth House	Evil.
Ninth House	Look for letters.
Tenth House	Good.
Eleventh House	Good in all.
Twelfth House	Very evil.

Chapter 8

AN EXAMPLE

Though the figures obtained on previous pages to describe the method of constructing the Mothers, Daughters and Nephews were chosen at random, totally unrelated at that time to any specifically formulated question, we will use them arbitrarily to refer to the hypothetical question raised a few pages back.

'Will *A Practical Guide to Geomantic Divination* be a publishing, educational and financial success to all concerned?' (Do remember, however, that no question was really asked while creating the initial geomantic symbols.)

1. The Significator is *Fortuna Minor* in the ninth house of publications. It represents good fortune and success. The textural interpretations say 'but choleric'. There will be some passions aroused by it publication.

2. It is trined by *Puer*–the dexter trine–a martial figure in the house of pleasure, ruling Aries. The fifth house is the natural house of Leo, both of them

being fiery signs. *Puer*, though tending to be rash, is nonetheless a sign of energy, of taking the initiative. The other trine is *Albus* in the first house. This is a mercurial figure quite clearly related to writing and publication: a very good figure. The total meaning is that the work will create pleasure for both author and publisher, and will new a new trail in the area of divinatory books.

3. It is square to *Rubeus* in the twelfth house, which is far from a good aspect. It indicates that secret enemies may attempt to harm the success of the book and malign it. It is also square to *Amisso* in the sixth house, which is far from a satisfactory figure.

4. It is sextile to *Via* in the seventh house, that of contracts, which is not a bad configuration for the publisher. It is sextile also to *Fortuna Major* in the 11th house, meaning that the book will make many friends far and wide for both author and publisher, and fulfil many of their hopes and wishes.

5. It is in opposition to the third house, also ruled by Gemini and Mercury. It contains *Caput Draconis*, which is a benign figure. No real opposition can therefore be expected.

6. The end of the matter is represented by *Laetitia*, in the fourth house. *Laetitia* is a Jupiterian figure, representing rejoicing and success. It speaks for itself.

To sum up briefly all these several factors, one could state that *A Practical Guide to Geomantic Divination* will be published, very soon, both author and publisher will be made happy over the way that the public receives it. The general public will find it instructive and useful, and the sales of the book should be very satisfactory, despite the effort of a few secret enemies of the author to decry and slander the book. It should be successful on most counts.

The Judge derived from the two witnesses is *Acquisitio*. This signifies that it need not be an overwhelming success in that it will never sell like a popular sex-novel: but it will sell well enough. The Reconciler would be *Carcer*–the addition of *Fortuna Minor* which is the Significator with the Judge which is *Acquisitio*. This indicates that it will reach a large number of people: which was the first intent of the author in writing the book, and the publisher in producing it. So all will go well, after some delays and setbacks.

From this example–and if the student really studies the preceding material and method–he should experience no major difficulty in making the method work. It is, as I have said, a most useful method for developing the psycho-spiritual factors, which the student should find of supreme value in his everyday life.

FINALE

The student would do well at the beginning to keep a notebook in which to enter the full reading of his interpretations. Later, as the divination is confirmed or proved incorrect or inadequate, he will be in a position to determine his accuracy in divination, or where he failed in his interpretations. This will also serve as an indicator of the emergence of his intuitive faculty. That is, it will prove if the intuition is working adequately or whether it is still dormant. It will also enable him to computer his percentage of success or failure. Then he may be able to confirm or otherwise what the writer and many others have found–some eighty-five per cent of accuracy in geomantic divination.

Chapter 9

ESSENTIAL DIGNITIES
From Vol. 5 of
The Golden Dawn Complete System of Magic

SIX

By essential dignity is meant the strength of a Figure when found in a particular House. A figure is, therefore, strongest when in what is called its house, very strong when its exaltation, strong in its Triplicity, very weak in its Fall; weakest of all in its Detriment. A figure is in its Fall when in a House opposite to that of its Exaltation, and in its Detriment when opposite to its own house.

The Geomantic figures, being attributed to the planets and Signs, are dignified according to the rules which obtain in Astrology. That is to say they follow the dignities of their ruling Planets, considering the Twelve Houses of the scheme as answering to the Twelve Signs. Thus, the Ascendant of First House answers to Aries, the Second House of Taurus, the Third House to Gemini, and so on to the Twelfth answering to Pisces. Therefore the figures of Mars will be strong in the First House, but weak in the Seventh House, and so forth.

TABLE OF DIGNITIES

Sign	Element	Ruler	Exaltation	Fall	Detriment	Strong
Aries	Fire	Mars	Sun	Saturn	Venus	Jupiter
Taurus	Earth	Venus	Luna	--	Mars	Jupiter
Gemini	Air	Mercury	--	--	Jupiter	Saturn
Cancer	Water	Luna	Jupiter	Mars	Saturn	Mercury
Leo	Fire	Sun	--	--	Saturn	Mars
Virgo	Earth	Mercury	Mercury	Venus	Jupiter	Saturn
Libra	Air	Venus	Saturn	Sun	Mars	Jupiter
Scorpio	Water	Mars	--	Luna	Venus	Sun
Sagittarius	Fire	Jupiter	--	--	Mercury	Venus
Capricorn	Earth	Saturn	Mars	Jupiter	Luna	Mercury
Aquarius	Air	Saturn	--	--	Sun	--
Pisces	Water	Jupiter	Venus	Mercury	Mercury	--

Caput Draconis is strong in the dignities of Jupiter and Venus.
Cauda Draconis is strong in the dignities of Saturn and Mars.

NOTES

The following notes were abstracted from a paper on Geomancy circulated in the A.O., which was the name given to the renewed Golden Dawn by Mathers years after the revolt. In it, the statement is made that it was compiled by S.R.M.D. from ancient treatises: 1) *Ye Geomancie of Maister Christopher Catton*; a very old work in black letters. 2) *The Theomagia by* John Heydon (17th century). 3) And the *Geomancia Astronomica* of Gerardus CAMBRENSIS or Cremonensis.)

In each set of four lines of print, the First or Top line is attributed to the element FIRE (as being the most subtle element), the second line to the Air (the next in lightness), the third to the Water (more heavy), and the fourth and lowest line to Earth (the heaviest of all).

Further that each set of Four points signifieth an element, thus:

The first Four Lines signify FIRE; the second Four the element AIR; the third Four lines the element of WATER; and the fourth Four lines the element of EARTH.

In Geomancy there are three points which may tend a little to confuse the Practicus: (a) Why the

Names and Seals of the SPIRITS of the Planets are employed instead of those of the INTELLIGENCIES, the former being said to be more Evil in nature, and the latter More Good. (b) This being so, why the names and sigils of the Archangels of the Zodiacal Signs, purely Good in Nature, should be also employed; and instead of those of either the Angels, or Assistant Angels of the Zodiac. (c) There being 16 figures of Geomancy, and these under the 12 Signs, how are the 4 extra to be attributed in this classification.

(a) Geomancy being a form of Divination especially attributed to the Element of Earth, and therefore more purely Terrestrial in operation, the Spirits and their Characters are more naturally appropriate hereto than the Intelligences, as representing the more weighty and automatic force of the Planetary Ray in its action upon the Earth. Also the Sigils employed in Geomancy are different from those of the same Spirits when taken from the Kameas of the Planes, and this to affirm their more specialized action in this Art.

(b) The reason of the employment of such powerful Names as those of Malchidael, etc., is to bring a strong aiding Force of Good into the Operation, again specialized by the Sigils used in this connection.

(c) The 12 Governors of the 12 Zodiacal Ideas or Figures, have power over the face of the Earth in their Figures and Places, but the 4 extra which be *Fortuna Minor*, *Via*, *Caput Draconis* and *Cauda Draconis*, also naturally have reference to the Four Winds and their Genii; a fortunate phase of the Moon (especially at Full) aspecting, is Good.

Gerardus Cremonensis sayeth:

But you must always take heed, that you do not make a Question in a Rainy, very Stormy, cloudy, or very Windy Season; that is when the Elements be Angry; or when thou thyself art angry, or thy mind over-busied with many affairs; nor for tempters nor deriders, neither renew nor reiterate the same question again under the same Figure or Form; for that is Error.

YE COMPANIE OF HOUSES
From the
Geomancie of Maister Christopher Cattan

When ye doe find a Good Figure in a good House, it is double Good, because the House is Good and the Figure also; and it signifieth that without any doubt the Querent shall obtain his Demand. By the like reason if ye find an Ill figure in an Ill House it is very Ill for the Querent. But if ye find a Good Figure in an Ill House, it signifieth Good to the Querent but it will not continue, but taken away part of the Malice of the House. In like case if ye find an Ill figure in a Good House, it taketh away the Malice of the Figure, for he would do harm, but he cannot; yet keeping back always the Good that it come not to the Querent.

By "Ill House" is meant that which in a Question shews persons or things opposed to the Querent or to his interest in the Question, as in a Lawsuit, The House shewing his Opponent; in a case of Sickness, the 6th and 8th would be hostile. "Good Houses" would be those shewing Aid etc. We might in a general sense consider the 6th and 8th, (death) and the 12th (Fears, prison, private enemies), "Ill House" by Nature.

The "Companie of the Houses" is after three manners: SIMPLE, SEMI SIMPLE, and COMPOUND. And the House be classed in Pairs, thus: the Second House is always the Companion of the First; the Fourth of the Third; the Sixth of the Fifth, and so on.

The COMPANIE SIMPLE is when the same Figure is repeated in both Houses of any of the "Pairs." Thus in our Scheme, *Via* is repeated in the PAIR formed by the Ascendant and the Second House and they are therefore in COMPANY together. In this case shew that the indecision of the querent re-acts on his business. But though *Caput Draconis* is repeated in the Fourth and Fifth houses which be next each other, there is no COMPANY, for they belong to different pairs, the Fourth house being the Companion of the Third and not of the Fifth, and the latter being Company to the Sixth and not to the Fourth. And with regard to Persons, the COMPANION Figure will shew the COMPANIONS or Associates of a Person in question, as also will the COMPANION House. Good Figures in COMPANY show much Good, and as well in the Present as in the time to come; and Evil Figures the reverse. For also the First House (of a Pair) showeth the Time Present, and the Second the Time to Come.

The COMPANY DEMI SIMPLE is when the Figures in the Two Houses forming a Pair be not identical, but be under the same Planetary Ruler as *Acquisitio* and *Laetitia* which be both under Jupiter and Hismael, *Fortuna Major* and *Minor* under the Sun. *Puella* and *Amissio* under Venus. etc.

The COMPANY COMPOUND is when the Points of the Two Figures be the exact complementary contrary one of the other in arrangement as *Puer* and *Puella, Albus* and *Rubeus, Acquisitio* and *Amissio*. *Laetitia* and *Tristitia*, etc. A Reconciler figure is then formed from them in the same way that the Judge is calculated from the Two Witnesses, and according as this Figure is harmonized with such and Good, so is the nature of this "Company Compound," but if discordant and evil so is this form of COMPANY.

There is also yet another kind of COMPANY which is that of the uppermost Line of the Two Figures in the Pair of Houses. If this uppermost line both cases be odd or even, there is COMPANY, and as in the case of the COMPANY COMPOUND, a Reconciler Figure is formed and the case judged as in the last paragraph. But if the top line of the one be odd and the other be even there is no COMPANY between those Figures. In our Scheme *Tristitia* is in the Third and *Caput* in the Fourth House, and as the top line of each has even points there is COMPANY between them. The Reconciler Figure will be *Conjunctio*, which is Harmonious with Both and is an argument of Good being signfied thereby.

The reference in the above to "our scheme" only means that Mathers had set up a divination in full, with its complete interpretation. I have not included it here because it would be redundant; one is already included in this text.

SEVEN

Remember always that if the figures *Rubeus* or *Cauda Draconis* fall in the Ascendant, or first house, the figure is not fit for Judgment and should be destroyed without consideration. Another figure for the question should not be erected before at least two hours have elapsed.

Your figure being thoroughly arranged as on a Map of the heavens, as previously shown, note first to what House the demand belongs. Then look for the Witnesses and the Judge, as to whether the latter is favourable or otherwise, and in what particular way.

Note next what Figure falls in the House of Houses. These should also be considered as for example in a question of money stolen, if the figure in the second House be also found in the sixth House, it might also show that the thief was a servant in the house.

Then look in the Table of Figures in the Houses and see what the Figure signifies in the special House under consideration. Put this down also. Then look in the Table for the strength of the figures in that House. Following this, apply the astrological rule of aspects between houses, noting what houses are Sextile, Quintile, Square, Trine, etc. Write the

"Good" on one side and the "Evil" on the other, noting also whether these figures also are "strong" or "weak," "friendly" or "unfriendly" in nature to the figure in the House required. Note that in looking up the aspects between houses, there are two directions. *Dexter* and *Sinister*. The *Dexter* aspect is that which is contrary to the natural succession of the houses; the *Sinister* is the reverse. The *Dexter* aspect is more powerful than the *Sinister*.

Then add the meaning of the figure in the Fourth House, which will signify the end of the matter. It may also assist you to form a Reconciler Figure from the Figure in the house required and the Judge, noting what figure results and whether it harmonises with either or both by nature. Now consider all you have written down, and according to the balance of "good" and "evil" therein form your final judgment.

Consider also in "money" matters where the Part of Fortune falls.

For example, let us consider the figure previously set up and form a judgment for "Loss of money in business" therefrom.

Populus is the Judge, and we find that in questions of money, which concern the Second

House, it signifies "medium good." The question as a whole is of the nature of the Second House, where we find *Carcer*. We then discover that *Carcer* here is "evil" as showing obstacles and delays. The Part of Fortune is in the Ascendant with *Amissio*, signifying loss through Querent's own mistake, and loss through Querent's self.

The Figure of *Amissio* springs into no other house, therefore this does not affect the question. "*Carcer*" in the Second House is neither "strong" nor "weak" its strength for evil is medium. The figures Sextile and Trine of the Second are *Conjunctio, Fortuna Major, Fortuna Minor*, and *Acquisitio*, all "good" figures, helping thc matter and "friendly" in nature. This signifies well intentioned help of friends. The figures square and opposition of the Second are *Fortuna Minor, Conjunctio, Albus* which are not hostile to *Carcer*, therefore showing "opposition not great."

The figure in the Fourth House is *Fortuna Major* which shows a good end but with anxiety. Let us know form a Reconciler between the figure of the Second House which is *Carcer* and the Judge, *Populus*, which produces *Carcer* again, a sympathetic figure, but noting delay, but helping the Querent's wishes. Now let us add all these together:

1. Medium.
2. Evil and Obstacles, delay.
3. Loss through querent's self.
4. Strength for evil, medium only.
5. Well-intentioned aid of friends.
6. Not much opposition from enemies.
7. Ending good; but with anxiety.
8. Delay, but helping Querent's wishes.

And we can formulate the final judgment. That the Querent's loss in business has been principally owing to his own mismanagement. That he will have a long and hard struggle, but will meet with help from friends. That his obstacles will gradually give way, and that after much anxiety he will eventually recoup himself from his former losses.

SUMMARY OF STAGES IN GEOMANTIC DIVINATION

1. If *Rubeus* or *Cauda Draconis* in Ascendant destroy the figure.
2. Note the House to which the question belongs. See if the figure there springs into another house.
3. Form the Judge from the two witnesses.
4. Part of Fortune that is, if a money question.
5. See if Figure in House concerned is "strong" or "weak." If it pass or spring into any other house.
6. See figures Sextile and Trine, Square and Opposition.
7. Friendly or unfriendly.
8. Note the figure in Fourth House, signifying the end or outcome.
9. Form the Reconciler from Judge and the figure in House to which the demand appertains.

New Falcon Publications
Publisher of Controversial Books and CDs
Invites You to Visit Our Website:
http://www.newfalcon.com

At the Falcon website you can:

- Browse the online catalog of all our great titles, including books by Robert Anton Wilson, Christopher S. Hyatt, Israel Regardie, Aleister Crowley, Timothy Leary, Osho, Lon Milo DuQuette and many more
- Find out what's available and what's out of stock
- Get special discounts
- Order our titles through our secure online server
- Find products not available anywhere else including:
    - One of a kind and limited availability products
    - Special packages
    - Special pricing
- And much, much more

Get online today at http://www.newfalcon.com